RUBANK EDUCATIONAL LIBRARY No. 94

Advanced Method

CORNET OR TRUMPET

VOL. I

WM. GOWER

AND

H. VOXMAN

AN OUTLINED COURSE OF STUDY
DESIGNED TO FOLLOW UP ANY
OF THE VARIOUS ELEMENTARY
AND INTERMEDIATE METHODS

RUBANK®

HAL•LEONARD®
CORPORATION
7777 W. BLUEMOUND RD. P.O. BOX 13819 MILWAUKEE, WI 53213

T0071552

NOTE

THE RUBANK ADVANCED METHOD for Cornet or Trumpet is published in two volumes, the course of study being divided in the following manner:

Vol. I
{ Keys of C, F, G, B♭, and D Major.
{ Keys of A, D, E, G, and B Minor.

Vol. II
{ Keys of E♭, A, A♭, E, D♭, and B Major.
{ Keys of C, F♯, F, and C♯ Minor.

PREFACE

THIS METHOD is designed to follow any of the various Elementary and Intermediate instruction series, or Elementary instruction series comprising two or more volumes, depending upon the previous development of the student. The authors have found it necessary in their teaching experience to draw from many sources in order to provide a progressive course of study. The present publication assembles in two volumes, the material essential to a well-rounded musical development.

THE OUTLINES, one of which is included in each of the respective volumes, tend to afford an objective picture of the student's progress. They will facilitate the ranking of members in a large ensemble or they may serve as a basis for awards of merit. In addition, a one-sided development along strictly technical or strictly melodic lines is avoided. The use of these outlines, however, is not imperative and they may be discarded at the discretion of the teacher.

Wm. Gower — H. Voxman

CHROMATIC FINGERING CHART
for Cornet and Trumpet

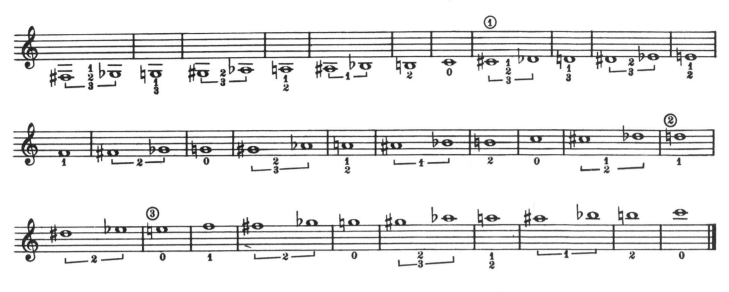

① The C♯ or D♭ below the staff is too sharp. Flatten this tone enough to make it in good tune.

② The D on the fourth line is usually too flat. In slow passages this may be improved by using the 1st and 3rd valves.

③ The E on the fourth space is sometimes too flat. Use the 1st and 2nd valves to correct this.

TABLE OF HARMONICS

Fingerings for the tones above high C:

PRACTICE AND GRADE REPORT

FIRST SEMESTER

Student's Name _____ Date _____

Week	Sun.	Mon.	Tue.	Wed.	Thu.	Fri.	Sat.	Total	Parent's Signature	Grade
1										
2										
3										
4										
5										
6										
7										
8										
9										
10										
11										
12										
13										
14										
15										
16										
17										
18										
19										
20										

Semester Grade _____

Instructor's Signature _____

SECOND SEMESTER

Student's Name _____ Date _____

Week	Sun.	Mon.	Tue.	Wed.	Thu.	Fri.	Sat.	Total	Parent's Signature	Grade
1										
2										
3										
4										
5										
6										
7										
8										
9										
10										
11										
12										
13										
14										
15										
16										
17										
18										
19										
20										

Semester Grade _____

Instructor's Signature _____

OUTLINE
OF
RUBANK ADVANCED METHOD
FOR
CORNET or TRUMPET, Vol. I
BY
Wm. Gower and H. Voxman

UNIT	SCALES and ARPEGGIOS	(Key)	MELODIC INTERPRETATION	ARTICULATION	FLEXIBILITY EXERCISES	ORNAMENTS	SOLOS	UNIT COMPLETED
1	6 (1) 7 (5)	C	18 (1)	46 (1)	56 (1)	59 (1)	65 (1)	
2	6 (2) 7 (6)	C	18 (2)	46 (2)	56 (1)	59 (1)	65 (1)	
3	6 (3) 7 (7)	C	19 (3)	46 (3)	56 (2)	59 (2)	65 (1)	
4	7 (4) (8)	C	20 (4)	47 (4)	56 (2)	59 (3)	65 (1)	
5	7 (9)	a	21 (5)	47 (5)	56 (3)	59 (4)	65 (1)	
6	7 (10) 8 (12)	a	21 (6)	47 (6)	56 (3)	59 (5)	65 (1)	
7	8 (11)	a	22 (7)	47 (7)	56 (4)	60 (6)	66 (2)	
8	8 (13) (14) (15)	a	22 (7)	47 (7)	56 (4)	60 (7)	66 (2)	
9	9 (16) 10 (20)	F	23 (8)	48 (8)	56 (5)	60 (8)	66 (2)	
10	9 (17) 10 (21)	F	24 (9)	48 (9)	56 (5)	60 (9)	66 (2)	
11	9 (18) 10 (22)	F	25 (10)	49 (10)	56 (6)	60 (9)	66 (2)	
12	9 (19)	F	25 (10)	49 (10)	56 (6)	61 (10)	66 (2)	
13	10 (23) (25)	d	26 (11)	49 (11)	56 (7)	61 (10)	67 (3)	
14	10 (24)	d	27 (12)	49 (12)	56 (7)	61 (11)	67 (3)	
15	10 (26) 11 (27) (28)	d	27 (12)	50 (13)	57 (8)	61 (12)	67 (3)	
16	11 (29) 12 (33)	G	28 (13)	50 (14)	57 (8)	61 (13)	67 (3)	
17	11 (30) 12 (34)	G	28 (13)	50 (15)	57 (9)	61 (14)	67 (3)	
18	11 (31) 12 (35)	G	30 (14) (15)	50 (15)	57 (9)	61 (15)	67 (3)	
19	11 (32) 12 (36)	G	31 (16)	51 (16)	57 (9)	62 (16)	68 (4)	
20	12 (37)	e	32 (17)	51 (17)	57 (10)	62 (17)	68 (4)	
21	12 (38)	e	33 (18)	51 (18)	57 (10)	62 (18) (19)	68 (4)	
22	13 (39) (40) (41)	e	33 (18)	52 (19)	57 (10)	62 (20)	68 (4)	
23	13 (42) 14 (46)	Bb	35 (19)	52 (20)	58 (11)	62 (21)	68 (4)	
24	13 (43) 14 (47)	Bb	35 (19)	52 (21)	58 (11)	62 (22)	68 (4)	
25	13 (44) 14 (48)	Bb	36 (20)	53 (22)	58 (12)	63 (23)	69 (5)	
26	14 (45)	Bb	36 (20)	53 (22)	58 (12)	63 (24)	69 (5)	
27	14 (49) 15 (53)	g	37 (21)	53 (23)	58 (13)	63 (25)	69 (5)	
28	14 (50) 15 (52) (54)	g	38 (22)	54 (24)	58 (13)	64 (26)	69 (5)	
29	14 (51)	g	38 (22)	54 (24)	58 (14)	64 (26)	69 (5)	
30	15 (55) 16 (59)	D	39 (23)	54 (25)	58 (14)	64 (27)	69 (5)	
31	16 (56) 17 (60)	D	39 (23)	54 (26)	58 (15)	64 (27)	71 (6)	
32	16 (57) 17 (61)	D	41 (24)	55 (27)	58 (15)	64 (28)	71 (6)	
33	16 (58) 17 (62)	D	41 (24)	55 (27)	58 (15)	64 (29)	71 (6)	
34	17 (63)	b	43 (25)	55 (28)	58 (15)	64 (30)	71 (6)	
35	17 (64)	b	44 (26)	55 (29)	58 (16)	64 (31)	71 (6)	
36	17 (65) (66) (67)	b	44 (26)	55 (29)	58 (16)	64 (32)	71 (6)	

NUMERALS designate page number.
ENCIRCLED NUMERALS designate exercise number.
COMPLETED EXERCISES may be indicated by crossing out the rings, thus, ⊗

Scales and Arpeggios
C Major

Various articulations may be used in the chromatic, the interval and the chord studies at the instructor's option.

Exercise in Thirds

Common Chord

Dominant 7th Chord

A Minor

The sign ∧ indicates a half-step

8

simile

simile

simile

simile

Exercise in Thirds

Common Chord

Diminished 7th

F Major

10

Thirds

20

Common Chord

21

Dominant 7th

22

D Minor

Natural **Harmonic**

23

Melodic

24

25

simile

simile

Thirds

26

Common Chord

27

Diminished 7th

28

G Major

29

30

31

32

33

Thirds
34

(123)

Common Chord
35

Dominant 7th
36

E Minor

Natural   **Harmonic**
37

Melodic

38

simile

Thirds

39

Common Chord

40

Diminished 7th

41

Bb Major

42

simile

simile

43

44

simile

45

46 Thirds

47 Common Chord

48 Dominant 7th

G Minor

49 Natural · Harmonic

Melodic

50

51

56

57

58

59

Thirds

60

Common Chord

61

Dominant 7th

62

B Minor

Natural   **Harmonic**

63

Melodic

64

Thirds

65

Common Chord

66

Diminished 7th

67

Studies in Melodic Interpretation
For One or Two Part Playing

The following studies are designed to aid in the development of the student's interpretative ability. Careful attention to the marks of expression is essential to effective use of the material. Pencil the technically difficult passages and devote extra time to their mastery.

In rhythmic music in the more rapid tempi (marches, dances, etc.) tones that are equal divisions of the beat are played somewhat detached (staccato.) Tones that equal a beat or are multiples of a beat are held full value. Tones followed by rests are usually held full value. This point should be especially observed in slow music.

BORTNIANSKY

HOHMANN

Moderato

3

GATTI

Allegretto

Tempo I

✱ trattenuto = ritardando

Andante religieux MARIE

Moderato MARIE

GATTI

Allegro giusto

7

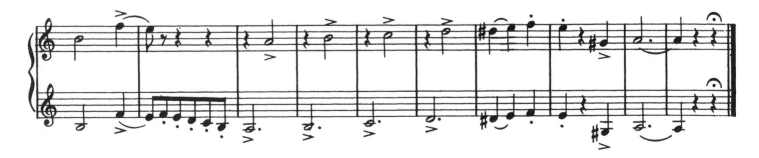

Moderato

SELTNER

SAINT-JACOME

NIEMANN

De GOUY

11

Tempo di bolero

Andante affettuoso

12

BONNISSEAU

Andantino grazioso

13

BONNISSEAU

CARNAUD

Valse (♩.=72)

14

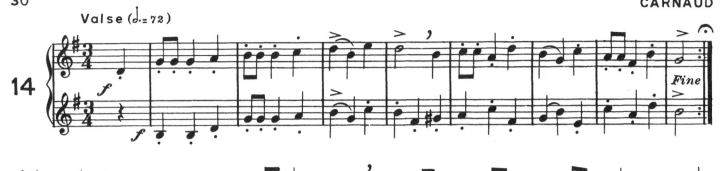

Allegro moderato

Folk Song

15

Allegretto grazioso

GATTI

16

Andante appassionato

17

GATTI

18

Andantino

GATTI

19

✷ *stentando = retarding the tempo.*

In No 20 play all detached eighth notes somewhat staccato

ST. JACOME

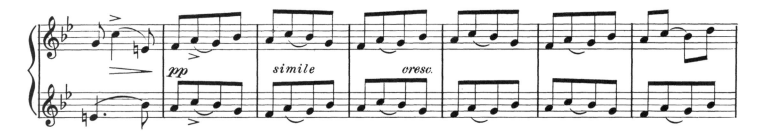

CARNAUD

Andante affetuoso (♩=66)

21

38

BONNISSEAU

22

GATTI

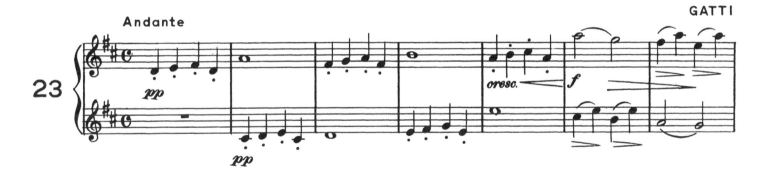

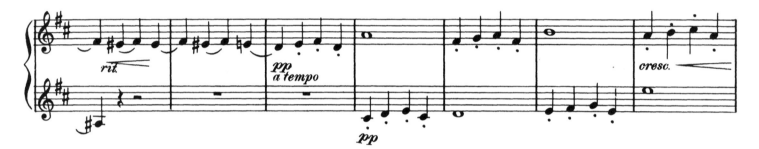

WAGNER

24

Marziale

Andante sostenuto

De GOUY

25

Andantino appassionato

26

* sonorously.
** accelerating.
*** *trattenuto* - same as ritardando.

Studies in Articulation

In all exercises where no tempo is indicated the student should play the study as rapidly as is consistent with tonal control and technical accuracy. The first practice on each exercise should be done very slowly in order that the articulation may be carefully observed.

In allegro tempi figures similar to  should be performed ,etc. The figure should be played

The material for these exercises has been taken from the methods of Arban, Gatti, St. Jacome, etc.

8

Moderato

9

13

14

15

19

20

sempre staccato

21

22

23

Flexibility Exercises

Keep the tone well sustained throughout the slur indicated, leaving no gaps between the tones. The slur must be made smoothly and evenly by the flexibility of the embouchure Adhere strictly to the fingerings given.

11

12

13

14

15

16

Musical Ornamentation (Embellishments)

The following treatment of ornamentation is by no means complete. It is presented here only as a guide to the execution of those ornaments which the student may encounter at this stage of his musical development. There are different manners of performing the same ornament.

The Trill (Shake)

The trill (or shake) consists of the rapid alternation of two tones. They are represented by the printed note (called the principal note) and the next tone above in the diatonic scale. The interval between the two tones may be either a half-step or a whole-step. The signs for the trill are *tr* and ⌇.

An accidental when used in conjunction with the trill sign affects the upper note of the trill.

Play as in No.1

Grace Notes (Appoggiatura)

The grace notes are indicated by notes of a smaller size. They may be divided into two classes: long and short.

Long grace notes

from "Serenade" Haydn

Andante cantabile

In instrumental music of recent composition the short grace notes should occupy as little time as possible and that value is taken preceding the principal note. They may be single, double, triple or quadruple, as the case may be. The single short grace note is printed as a small eighth note with a stroke through its hook.   It is not to be accented. Use trill fingerings when fundamental fingerings are too difficult.

Short grace notes

Allegretto   ARBAN

The Mordent

The short mordent (𝄽) consists of a single rapid alternation of the principal note with its lower auxiliary. Two or more alternations are executed in the long mordent.

The inverted mordent (𝄽) does not have the cross line. In it the lower auxiliary is replaced by the upper. It is the more commonly used mordent in music for the wind instruments.

The mordent takes its value from the principal note.

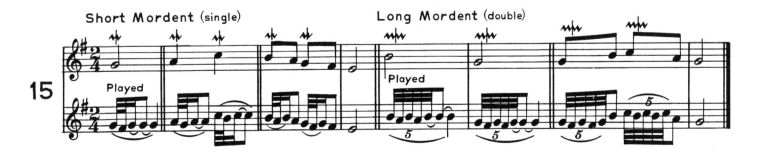

Short Inverted Mordent   **Long Inverted Mordent**

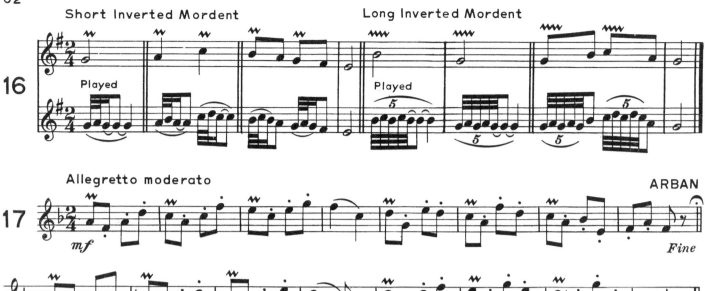

16

Allegretto moderato

ARBAN

17

mf

Fine

D.C. al Fine

In trills of sufficient length a special ending is generally used whether indicated or not

The closing of the trill consists of two tones: the scale tone below the principal note and the principal note.

In long trills of a solo character, it is good taste to commence slowly and gradually increase the speed. Practice the following exercises in the manner of both examples 1 and 2.

Ex.1   **Ex.2**

18

Played

19

20

21

22

The Turn (Gruppetto)

The turn consists of four tones: the next scale tone above the principal tone, the principal tone itself, the tone below the principal tone, and the principal tone again.

When the turn ∾ is placed to the right of the note, the principal tone is held almost to its full value, then the turn is played just before the next melody tone. In this case (Ex. 1, 2, 3, 4, and 5) the four tones are of equal length.

When the turn is placed between a dotted note and another note having the same value as the dot (Ex. 6 and 8), the turn is then played with the last note of the turn taking the place of the dot, making two notes of the same value. The turn sign after a dotted note will indicate that one melody note lies hidden in the dot.

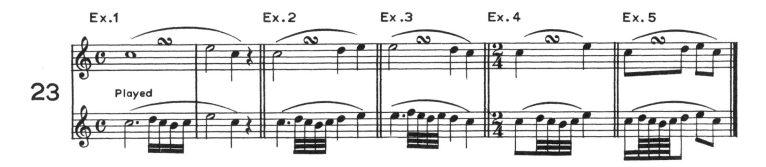

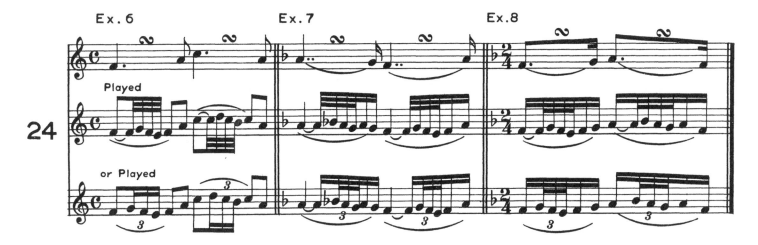

Sometimes an accidental sign occurs with the turn, and in this case when written above the sign, it refers to the highest tone of the turn, but when written below, to the lowest. (Ex. 2 and 1 below).

When the turn is placed over a note (Ex. 3) the tones are usually played quickly, and the fourth tone is then held until the time value of the note has expired.

In the inverted turn (Ex. 4) the order of tones is reversed, the lowest one coming first, the principal next, the highest third and the principal tone again, last. The inverted turn is indicated by the ordinary turn sign reversed: ∾ or by ⌇.

64

Allegretto

26

Andante

27

28

29

30

31

32

Calm As the Night

BOHM

Shepherds Dream

B♭ Trumpet (Solo)
Cornet - Bar.

C. H. TAYLOR

Copyright MCMXXIX by Rubank Inc., Chicago, Ill.
International Copyright Secured

Cantique de Noel
(O Holy Night)

Solo B♭ Cornet (or Trumpet)

ADOLPHE ADAM
Transcribed by G.E. Holmes

Copyright MCMXXXIX by Rubank Inc.,Chicago, Ill.
International Copyright Secured

CENTAURUS

VANDER COOK

Copyright MCMXXXVIII by Rubank Inc. Chicago, Ill.
International Copyright Secured

ARCTURUS

VANDER COOK

Copyright MCMXXXVIII by Rubank Inc. Chicago, Ill.
International Copyright Secured

70

TRiO

Moderato

Vivace

Arcturus

RIGEL

VANDER COOK

TRIO

Rigal